"Please forgive me… I can't stop loving you."

Bryan Adams.

And so it starts…

I want retribution for this smile you bring out of me every day. Don't hold back. Yours is my win.

Dreams…

Some dreams are disguised as memories, or maybe some memories are so extraordinary that one may wonder if one was dreaming. I can dive into either and not tell them apart, and it feels amazing. May all your dreams become extraordinary memories.

Blue…

I had never been so attracted to blue. I guess it brings me back to places I didn't want to leave.

Happy ending…

I wanted our story to have a happy never-ending. Instead, it had a bittersweet non-start. It is, however, eternal.

Details…

You make every detail count… with a magnifying glass.

Showing up…

There is something magic about showing up. It doesn't matter how tired, scared, or insecure we are, when we still show up regardless, it's like the universe rewards us for being brave, and gift us with unimaginable treasures. When I saw you standing there at the airport, I knew I was about to be amazed. I am so thankful to myself for showing up that day.

Purpose…

Even when the crystal is not clear, you can still see the sun coming out through the dirt, cloudiness, and remains of rain splash. Open the window and you will feel the light. You are closer, you are here, you are alive. Open your eyes. Live with purpose.

Ocean…

The deep blue, the breeze, the soothing sound of the waves kissing the shore, the calm, the peace, the immensity and mystery… It is impossible to not be seduced by the ocean. New love has the same effect. The endless possibilities, the rush, the butterflies, the high, the ectasis are hypnotizing; but just as the ocean, when the storms roar, the waves hit the rocks so hard the world seems to be shaken, the sky reflects the darkness of unsettled waters fighting inner battles, it can be scary and devastating. Nevertheless, we keep going back to the ocean, we can't stay away.

Uncertainty…

Humans avoid uncertainty, only to miss the times when not knowing what would happen was actually a bliss. Then certainty comes and ruins the countless dreams.

Fear…

Fear is paralyzing, it's debilitating, but it is just a fog whose only danger is to not let us see forward. Fear creates monsters and disasters, and all sorts of catastrophes that reduce our mind and our will to a cornered rabbit, who does not realize that the doors to freedom are wide open, if only it would walk through the fog.

Truth...

This distance entertains my hope. It gives me a sense of safety because there is a reason why this love I had only seen in movies, cannot become. I hide behind the obstacles and rest my back against them while I rejoice in the fact that someone else is at fault, that you would choose me if the path was clear. Then this unwelcome, insolent thought comes to poison my serenity, and calls itself "truth". This thought disrupts my clueless hope, cutting right through this sweet abyss of denial and screams in a whisper: You are a fantasy diversion on his path, a pretty landscape that appeared in front of a man with dreams of freedom, but prisoner of his fears. His road doesn't lead to you. His fears pull harder than your oasis of freedom in the middle of the desert, where he won't build a home. He needs firm ground, and you are sand.

Lost...

Fire. Heat. Electricity. Who cares... energy that possesses my whole body with just the hint of a thought. Maybe your unexpected touch, a smile that takes me hostage, the smell of your sweat and my desire, my hands that can feel you intensely navigating my darkest pieces of paradise. I am so lost in you. And I don't want to be found.

Shadows…

Why can I not grow old with you, next to you, behind you, in front of you, and in every position life puts us every step of the way? Or is it my destiny to live in the shadows of a life that is not mine? But if I can inspire a smile and a whim of hope, if I can push you to be the best you, if I can make you happy one more day… There is no question, I will stay.

Breath…

It hurts so much it takes my breath away. It burns so deep it takes my breath away. It's so intense it takes my breath away. I'm not breathing half the time, yet I've never felt so alive.

Pictures…

Pictures immortalize moments, and revive the memories, almost gifting us the most valuable treasure: time. Pictures also show intentions, sceneries that one wants to perpetuate because they are statements: happy family, enjoyment, love, partnership, accomplishments, grief, admiration. Pictures are revealing, even more so for those who are not in them.

Drops…

The weight of this unstoppable, growing love is cracking my soul, and all I can do is release little drops at a time when I get to have you in my arms for a fleeting moment that slips away, a little faster every time.

Envy…

Jealousy has nothing on this pure envy that I feel when I think about who gets to touch you, watch you sleep, kiss you until it hurts, make plans with you, build a home with you, enjoy your smile, fall in love with you over, and over again. And it's not sharing you what bothers me, because your heart is mine and I can feel it. It is this cruel realization that it should be me doing all that, and who can do it, isn't at all.

Tools…

I see my dreams, our dreams, crumble in front of my eyes as I fly away. And I'm already thinking of the tools I need to put them back together. I'm not ready to give up, so let me have one smile, one touch, one kiss and I will be, once again, holding on to this almost nothing that is so much, so powerful, or enough to become the foundation of my dreams, our dreams. I'll do it for both, just let me have the tools.

You...

Why do I love you this much? How did I fall so hard? What do I do with this tormenting need to be yours? When does it stop? Where do I place it if it can't be on you? Tell me, love, why can't I have you?

Epic...

I love you. And it's painful, but in a way that doesn't push me away. See, I knew when I met you that you were not for me, but the way you've healed me opened my heart to the possibility of epic love, of selfless love. I know I need to let you go, and I will, but my love is not fragile, so it will stay even after I'm gone. So, I will leave, but you can keep my love. It was meant for you, it belongs with you.

Timing...

I would love to stay. I dream about white sand, family portraits, idyllic discoveries, kisses in forbidden places, anatomically and geographically. I would dedicate my life to your happiness and my energy to your fulfillment. But I must go, before the reality of your place, of my place, breaks my soul in so many pieces that you can't find me if you ever come looking. I must go to stay whole, because my heart beats for that one day when you wake up and decide it's time to come find me.

Flame…

One day you asked me to keep your cigar alight. I took that to heart, and right then and there I knew I would do anything to keep this flame alight. I will, rest assured my love, this fire cannot die.

Walls…

And then I met you. And I tore my walls down so you could come in and see everything, and I was so sure you would run away. But then you loved me, and in so doing, you introduced me to myself.

Helpless…

As I saw you there, smiling at me under a nervous mask, I was shaking with excitement. And the first time I smelled your skin I knew I was helpless. And then we went up to the top of the world and we ignored the fall. In that moment, we were forever.

Smile…

Your smile disarms me. It leaves me floating in a cloud of wet desires. It pulls me into the powerful spell of your eyes' language, which strips me to the core and makes love to all of me with just one look. Your smile was all I needed to fall in love, but then you kissed me, and my heart did not stand a chance.

Home…

I never wanted to fall in love with a man that was taken. Has anyone ever wanted such a thing? I never wanted to fall in love at all. But you came along and healed my heart unexpectedly, only to break it again, and again, and again. But this time, this time it was worth it because, well, you brought me back to life and reminded me that my heart is capable of feeling and burning for that touch, that sound, that look that makes it beat out of my chest. This time I knew the heartbreak was coming, but I didn't guard myself, I was too immersed in all this happiness, all these emotions, all these extraordinary sensations I didn't know I was capable of. I was flooded with your love, and I was not drowning. I was complete, I was yours, I was home.

Magic…

Kissing you was magic. You used to wish me magic days and all I could think of was, "if only I could kiss you, I'd have my magic". I don't know if I will ever have it again, so I close my eyes and kiss you in my mind, and I can feel the sparkles, the colors, the fireworks. And then I beg the universe for one more moment of your magic.

Gravity…

True love is like gravity. No matter how high you jump, how hard you push, how much you try, you will always be pulled back. Even if you manage to get out to a space so far away where it doesn't have an effect on you, there will always be a certainty that if you come close enough, you will fall again.

Pieces…

I was always hoping it would hurt less every time we said goodbye until the time I would no longer care. Instead, every time it hurt more, because my love was bigger by the day, so there would be more shattered pieces with every break.

Principles...

Loving a man with principles very often means competing against their idea of what's right, even if that's in the opposite direction of what they desire the most. And how can you resent someone that is so selfless, that would relinquish the rare chance at true love for what they perceive as the greater good? Loving a man with principles is having the utmost admiration for what will in fact, break your heart.

Yours...

I knew you were not for me and it was dangerous to love you. But one smile was too many and too late. I loved you anyway, because I was already yours.

Bittersweet...

Have you ever loved someone so much it hurts to breathe, and walked away from it? I had never experienced such a bittersweet pain. Our souls were holding on to each other, but we had to part ways. Someone, please take your fist out of my chest.

Marks…

A mark on your skin is a visible accessory, or a permanent reminder of something meaningful. A mark on your soul becomes a piece of your essence, a building block of your inner self. Even when the memories fade, the effect of such mark remains, shapes, defines, creates, transcends. I have both from you, and you are forever with me.

Glimpse…

I got a glimpse of what my life would be with you; and I adored every piece of that dream. I have no idea of what it will be without you; but I know that, after you, it will never be the same.

Biblical…

I love you, I knew it long before you did. I whispered it every time I read your name. And I knew you could feel it, but I needed to say it, so I did. I had never felt so exposed and so embraced, so brave and so scared, so certain, so selfish, so excited, so empowered, and so vulnerable. And then you said it back, and you erased all of my conflicts, and it was… biblical.

Battles…

I would fight a million battles for one last kiss, with the same courage that I would walk away to spare your pain, even if that means taking it all in.

Burden…

I don't know what I wouldn't do for you. Here I am, loving you like I do, and disappearing from your life so you don't have to carry this burden of loving me from afar.

Possibilities…

There is a parallel universe in which you ask and I say yes, in which it doesn't hurt to love you so purely, in which you surpass your fears and discover a world of possibilities. There is a parallel universe in which we choose to be free, and make our dreams never stop.

Goodbye…

How can you say goodbye to the love of your life, knowing that you mean the same to him? How do you tell your heart that you need to stop giving him this exhilarating life he was getting? How do you walk away from what has kept you alive for what would have been the most miserable year of your life otherwise?

Last time…

If I had known that was the last time I would make love to you, I would have kissed you longer, I would have touched you harder, I would have breathed every second of your presence. I would have not been enough, but I would have been conscious about losing you, I would have said I love you a million times and hugged you until we became one.

Always…

If you don't hear from me ever again, just know I will love you beyond life, that you will forever be the one I never had, but the place where I belong. If you don't hear from me ever again, I hope you know that there will be a space in my life for you, always.

Break…

I want to cry until my soul dies and is born again. I have a strange need to feel this pain of losing you because what if the last time I get to feel something so deep and real? I don't care if this will break me to the point of no return. I'd rather break for you forever than watch this love fade away and out of my heart. Break me in pieces, but stay in me, don't let me lose the memories too.

Deja-voo…

Losing someone is a very painful experience, but also joyful once the winds of the soul settle and become a breeze. Then what shook you up amid a storm becomes a gentle caress that brings along a quiet satisfaction, a deja-voo of remarkable instances when your whole body was immersed in a religious experience, in an ecstatic trance you didn't quite understand at the time. Now you get to relive it and enjoy it over, and over again. And then you are grateful that the universe gifted you such a unique adventure you got to share with this person that will be a part of you forevermore.

Her…

She and I are two of the same. We hold on desperately to the hope that something will happen, that will make the other one go away.

Memories…

I can hear your heart beating desperately when the touch of my lips visits your memories unexpectedly. I can hear it when my head rests on your chest, as we meet in that same memory. Or is it a dream?

Quit…

I never thought it would be so hard to quit love… much less to kill it when it refuses to die but there is no place for it where it wants to go. Maybe I can't, maybe I need to hide it forever until it starves or until there is a life where it's intended to flourish.

Conflicts…

I was chasing a dream that wasn't mine to have and I wouldn't take no for an answer. Yes, it is inspiring to have the kind of spirit that will ignore and break barriers to achieve a dream, but the price is high for chasing the wrong one. There is pain, and tears, and resentment, and neglect, and conflicts, and confusion, and this overall feeling of wrongness all the time, except when, for one glorious minute, you get to feel that dream, touch it, and believe it true. Then you don't care what it will take… you will do anything to have at least that magic minute.

Nothing…

First it was nothing, then a tingling in my fingers at the sound of a message. Then there were expectations of that sound every day. Then there was one kiss, and crumbs - and that was enough, until it wasn't. Then there were hopes of a next time, a sunrise, another hour, another day. Then there were dreams of a future that was impossible, then there were plans to erase the word “impossible”. Then dreams became goals of a life, a home, a family, only this time the goals were one-sided. Then there was reality, and inertia, and fears, and conflicts. Then there were broken dreams, but stubborn hopes, and hidden kisses, and trips, and whole days with its nights. Then there were crumbs again, and sad realizations that brought us back to nothing.

Course…

Call me a crazy utopist, but I firmly believe that walking away from this will have more detrimental outcomes than staying. So I won't, I will happily bear the blame so the flower gets to thrive - or not- by its natural course.

Jump...

No, I didn't knock on that door, I didn't ask for permission, I didn't bring a checklist to make sure it was ok. But who does? The most amazing experiences are those where a man jumps at an opportunity that gives him a gut feeling that this is where he is supposed to be, and he breaks through the discomfort. Life is just a collection of decisions... so what happens if you stay still and make no decisions? Then life happens FOR you, not TO you. I saw a very small, almost concealed opening and I walked right into a situation that was less than ideal, but love flourished, nevertheless. I am amazed at the desert flowers. They grow and thrive in the middle of rocks and gravel. Who can then come and tell that flower that has managed to blossom unapologetically, that she doesn't get to live because of some rules that apparently ignore the relevance of love and uniqueness?

Consequences...

I can't walk away. No matter how hard I try - because humans tend to perpetuate their liability entitlement. They need to summon the word "consequences" in a negative light, they need to be painfully aware of what can go wrong and who is at fault. I try to walk away because I have been forced to learn that if I keep going a child will end up without a father, a family will be broken, a woman will be left alone and will be stolen from her love, and I will carry the blame and name-calling. But as much as I try to get these societal stigmas in my head and walk away I can't. See, my insolent, daring, free and rebel mind has its own story going on and it impairs my ability to go against it: I have found true, selfless, intense, passionate, beautiful love that is worth pursuing, and if I keep going two children will end up with a bonus dad and a bonus mom, and a network of loving caretakers. A woman will not settle for a mediocre love which is more inertia and co-dependency than anything else. She might go on to fulfill her untapped potential and find the amazing love she deserves. She will be freed from her fears, and so will a man who has a free soul, but a prisoner mind. This man will still be the wonderful father he is, will enjoy this epic love that has touched his heart so unexpectedly, will teach his daughter to be brave and chase her dreams, will not grow old and bitter with resentment because he didn't dare, will achieve greatness because he will be inspired. Dreams will come true, memories will be created, love will heal wounds and create a massive structure with an unshakeable foundation.

Leaving…

Why did I leave then? Why didn't I leave sooner? I knew you were not coming after me, it was me chasing a dream that died before having the chance to live. I should I left sooner when it didn't hurt so much. You would have stayed still either way, but I would have been less broken. I waited to leave, and now I can't stop this urge to beg you, please let me come back.

Christmas…

If someone had told me that Christmas would be grey, and sad, and somber that year, I would have said: impossible. The dreams I had built, the happiness I couldn't shake off, the plans, the illusions, the excitement… we were finally free to live our story. But life had other plans, and I learned the hard way that I was deep up to my neck in the ocean of our story, and you were just testing the waters.

Crumbling…

I am wearing something that smells like your bed. I'm also wearing my soul inside out. Our forever is cracking and crumbling, and my soul can't bear another tear, so I have it out in hopes it will dry before it breaks. I pray it won't shrink away, like the dreams of you.

Smell…

I can't undo my bag. I need to preserve your smell in every piece of dirty clothes. That's all I have left from you now. Memories, flashbacks, tears, regrets and the smell of our love that brings me back to your arms, piece by piece, day after day.

Save me…

I desperately need to hear that promised knock on my door. I know it won't happen, but how much it would save me right now. I desperately need to love you again, for that last kiss I can't quite remember. I need to kiss you with purpose, I need to remember every second of it so I can go back to it until it doesn't hurt anymore.

Sunsets…

I miss you so much. It hurts to look at your pictures as it hurts to look at a sunset. And you know how much I love sunsets. But I sought refuge from the pain of our goodbye on the sunsets that could not bring me peace, only nostalgia. Now sunsets will always be a little painful.

Wounds…

How do you heal from a wound that was supposed to happen much later? You know you will get hurt but you push it, and ignore the certainty you feel in your gut, telling you that it's coming… But you don't want to listen because you are happy. How do you heal from a cut you knew you'd get, but when you cut yourself, you wish you had pushed it further, even knowing that it would be irreparable later?

Promise…

"I promise"… is what you said when I asked you once to come back for me. I will never stop waiting. I will never give up, and that I promise you.

Again…

The pain was not enough to keep me away. My resiliency scares me because I tend to expose myself to situations that will hurt me, juts because I can handle it. My heart wants to jump out of my chest when I see your face, even being thousands of miles away. I can feel your love and I can't help to be drawn in one more time. The hits I thought I could not survive, became distant and vague memories. Again, I run to you, and I see it in your eyes that you await with a desperate craving of my touch. And here I go, unapologetically, unafraid, fully committed, again.

Darkness…

Driving through a storm can be very unpredictable. We may see the darkness ahead, we may anticipate bad weather, but we don't know for certain for how long it will rain, how hard, how much wind, or if the storm will fade before a rain drop falls. More often than not, we don't have a choice, we can't turn back. So we drive, and hope for the best, knowing that we could have to face the worst. After all, we could see the darkness ahead, and we know there will be sunlight again, so we drive right through it.

Back to her…

Her pain is not less than mine, it is probably worse. Her ability to push through the chaos is admirable. I don't know if that is pure manipulation, or resiliency. But how can I resent someone that is simply living her story, navigating her disaster, trying to keep her ship afloat to the best of her ability. I can't blame her, I am also fighting to keep you, and we share nothing more than a torrid affair. If you were my family, I don't know what I wouldn't do if a "me" comes along. She has my respect. I don't know if I can say the same about you.

Backlash…

I didn't mean to hurt her, but I did. I didn't mean to hurt me, but I did. I didn't mean to hurt my loved ones by exposing them to this version of me that they can't handle, but I did. But you hurt me like none and nothing before, so I wanted to hurt you back with all of me, and I knew just the right way. I did not hesitate because I love you too much, and I knew I needed to push you way as far as possible, or this cycle of morbid control and possessiveness, this game of powers and passions, would never end. So I did…

Mine…

I will never get to call you mine, and I don't know if I will ever get over it, over you, but I will go back to the dreams of you being mine, as if they were memories. I don't care if they never happened, I will remember them as if my life was tied to yours in another life.

Last kiss…

I need to disappear. I can't keep waiting for something that will never happen... like you showing up for me, once, even if it's one last time. I have to accept the last kiss was actually the last.

Enough…

I'd rather think you are a coward, and not that you didn't want me enough to take a few risks, or a plane, or just the phone without asking. I would have been going to you time and again, and again, and again.

Hurt…

I wish you did something once, because it is what you want even if it doesn't make sense. I wished so much that you chased what you wanted at least once, and I wished that something was me. But I pushed, I forced everything, I made myself available to make it easy for you, and it hurts so much to know that you didn't want it as much as I did.

Knife…

I keep telling myself you broke my heart, but I did that to myself... I put myself in front of the knife, and I pushed.

Gone…

It will be very easy to have me if I also want you, because I go for what I want relentlessly. It will be easy to retain me if I want to stay because I will give myself to you, wholly and unconditionally. It will not be as easy to lose me if I don't want to leave, because I will try everything to see us be, and remain. But if you lose me baby, you will have to go beyond the ends of the world to even find me again, because I will be out of reach, even if visible, I will be untouchable, even if within reach, I will be gone, even if present. If you lose me, there is no guarantee that I will ever be yours again, even if my heart desires nothing more than to see you come for me.

Luna…

A year ago today the world became a better, brighter place... I already had my sun, and then my moon came out, and I was in love forever. Happy birthday little queen. May you be fearless but patient, strong but vulnerable, brave but cautious, caring but guarded, ambitious but humble, and may you always feel how loved you are.

Signs…

One more sign… after a long silence. One more hint, that doesn't let me forget the burning sensation of your grip. One more hidden message, my heart wants to escape my body and my desperation brings me to my knees and I give in to your calling. And I see the fairy knocking at my door… let me build a castle for you, let me paint this story, let me give you a taste of happy ever after. Then the voices in your head paint you the worst version of me, and you don't hesitate to listen, and once again I am a stranger looking into a life that will never be mine. Then another sign, and I can't help to open the window, but you never jump in, you just peak and hide behind the huge pile of fears.

Translation…

Your love confuses me. I don't understand its twists and turns. Your love speaks one language, but acts another, and I don't know how to fix the translation. Maybe I don't want to take it at face value, and keep hoping it's missing the message, because it can't be right. Love can't be so fragile; I can't be so wrong.

Desperation…

Tears were coming down my face as I reached the peak of our love act, which transported me to another dimension, always. Your touch was really magic, and I purposely felt every second of you that night. I tried so hard to hold on to every piece of my reality, your eyes, your smell, your voice, your face, your smile… oh, your smile. I knew the end was coming, I wasn't sure when, but I cried for you as much as I reached, and I could not keep you. Desperation had never felt so helpless.

Faith…

Faith is something powerful. Faith can move men to do the unthinkable. Good faith is like an engine… well maintained it will go to great lengths, but it will stop if neglected. Bad faith is like an engine just as powerful. The difference is, it needs less maintenance, it can last longer, and it dies harder. Good faith is an engine moving you forward, whereas bad faith is an engine pulling you down to an abyss of ghosts that will consume your soul and convince you that your shadow is out to kill you, your feet are out to make you trip, and your walls are closing in, when the reality may be quite the opposite.

Doomed…

What if love is meant to be felt, but not truly lived? What if love is too consuming, too blinding, and we are just meant to have a taste of it, but not enough to be fully satisfied? What if love is meant to be chased but never found, only barely touched when it's passing us by and we can see it, feel it, but not really retain it? Will we be wandering through life trying to emulate that fleeting moment? Will we be forever doomed to hunt something that never stays?

Undying Love....

It's been a while since I don't come here, where my thoughts become words I can come back to later. The inevitable distance has turned our story into a box in the back of the closet, full of pictures, letters, and memorabilia. I forget it's there sometimes, and even feel guilty when days go by and I don't think of you, of us. But some days I run to the box, get everything out, kiss the pictures and cry over the lost sunsets. Then I put it back and smile. Nothing can take away the happiness in the box, and it's ours, and for that I am forever grateful. Maybe one day you will fulfill your promise and come find me, maybe one day we'll have the castle. Until then, I say to you, my undying love that never was, nobody will ever love you like I have. I hope you are the happiest you can be, but I also hope you never stop smiling and feeling my touch when you drive down the strip, and I am next to you, completely paralyzed by your perfection and hypnotized by your voice, interrupting you to say: I'm so in love with you. Know that I would do it all again, no questions asked, for I am as certain as I am alive, you are the love of my life.

The End...

Wait... incoming message.

Maybe not, maybe not yet.

www.ingramcontent.com/pod-product-compliance
Lightning Source LLC
LaVergne TN
LVHW052114160826
845678LV00015B/3554

* 9 7 9 8 3 5 2 4 1 0 7 8 3 *